THE SECRET BEHIND WEALTH

BLUEPRINT FOR BUILDING AND STAYING IN WEALTH

All rights reserved. No part of this publication may be reproduced, distributed, or transmitted in any form or by any means, including photocopying, recording, or other electronic or mechanical methods, without the prior written permission of the publisher, except in the case of brief quotations embodied in critical reviews and certain other noncommercial uses permitted by copyright law.

Copyright © Harry K. Wiggins 2022

Table of Contents

Chapter 1
What Is Wealth Building?

Chapter 2
Smart Strategies For Building Wealth

Chapter 3
Overcoming Obstacles To Wealth

Chapter 4
Staying In Wealth

Introduction

Getting wealthy is very high on most people's list of financial dreams and aspirations. After all, it will enable you to not only have greater financial stability but also have more possibilities. And, of course, you would have the capacity to spend on more of the things you desire.

The issue with the concept of being "rich," however, is that it takes a lot of time and work. Get-rich-quick scams are nearly usually nothing but a method to prey on individuals who are suffering financially. Unless you are born into a wealthy family and a big inheritance is transferred to you, you will likely have to become rich via a mix of hard work and financial vigilance.

It may seem implausible to some people, but it doesn't have to be an out-of-reach pipe dream. With careful planning, perseverance,

and smart savings, you can easily earn a million dollars by the time you retire.
You don't need a six-figure career or family money to become a billionaire. Instead, you need to start saving early and be aware of every dollar you spend.

Building money may be one of the most exciting and gratifying tasks in a person's life. Aside from giving a more pleasant day-to-day experience, considerable net worth may relieve stress and anxiety by relieving you from concern about putting food on the table or being able to pay your expenses.

For others, that alone is enough incentive to start the financial path. For others, it's more like a game, and their love for wealth creation starts with their first dividend check from a company they own, interest deposit from a bond they purchased, or rent check from a renter living in their property.

While there are innumerable articles devoted to various approaches and strategies for generating money and getting rich, the guidance below focuses more generally on the idea underlying how to become affluent. Considering these principles might help you better comprehend the nature of the problem you confront when you set to the process of creating excess money.

Chapter 1

WHAT IS "WEALTH-BUILDING?"

Wealth building is the process of producing long-term revenue from many sources. This refers to more than job-based income and instead covers savings, investments, and any income-generating assets. The wealth-building definition depends on adequate financial planning and insight into one's future financial objectives. Many people will turn to wealth development as a strategy to assure a good financial future.

To grow wealth over time, you must follow three basic steps: earn money, save money, and invest money. Before investing, it is crucial to establish a dependable income stream that covers your long-term financial future. After a solid source of income is confirmed, it is important to develop a precise savings strategy. Finally, it is time to invest.

1. Making Money

This stage may seem simple, but it is necessary to mention that a steady source of solid income throughout time is crucial to wealth-building. A little sum of consistent savings from this source of income may compound into a considerable quantity. A crucial thing to ask yourself is whether or not your present employment can give you a consistent quantity of money for 40 to 50 years. If not, it may be time to seek methods to boost your income.

The two main forms of income are earned and passive. Earned money comes from your normal profession, whereas passive income comes from investments. To raise your earning income, you may first have to make adjustments in your profession. If you're pondering a career shift, ask yourself these questions to assist you to decide on your new position. To begin, what do you love doing, and what talents are you naturally excellent at? Finding a career that corresponds with areas in which you excel and tasks that you like will automatically help you to perform better and start raising your income. Of course, you'll also want to be sure that your chosen vocation will pay well. Consider investing in your schooling and other types of training to help you become a better contender for your chosen career.

Once you reach the right financial stability, you can start saving and investing.

2. Saving Money
Many individuals live well after attaining financial security, however, they still don't save their money wisely. The second element of wealth-building is saving away a percentage of your earned money consistently. Once you have saved enough, you may start investing to create passive income. Here are a few methods you to start saving money:

Keep track of your expenditure each month, and then crowd out the products, services, and experiences that you don't truly need.

Adjust your budget as your experiment to the point in which you're saving every month, but also aren't denying yourself to the point that living isn't pleasurable.

Always have roughly 6 months' worth of spending saved in case of crises. Having a buffer can help prevent you from derailing your finances every time something unexpected arises.

Contribute to your retirement plan. If your workplace has a matching plan, certainly take advantage of it. Don't leave free money on the table.

3. Investing Money
Finally, after you have a firm basis, you may start investing your money. However, to establish a broad investment portfolio, you

will have to take a few risks. It is crucial to examine how much asset allocation is optimal for you. While you may perform this research yourself, engaging a financial counselor is also suggested for beginning investors.

They may help you get clarity on your investment objectives, time horizon, and how much risk you can bear. Depending on these insights, they may help you construct a diversified portfolio that is risk-averse, moderate, or aggressive, based on your preferences.

The answer to "what is wealth building" is vital for everyone trying to enhance their present income. By constructing a wealth development method, entrepreneurs may create a profitable investment portfolio and attain financial independence.

Choosing the correct wealth-building assets comes down to which possibilities best fit your financial objectives. With the appropriate strategy, potential investors may be well on their way to producing wealth via real estate and other assets.

Chapter 2
SMART STRATEGIES FOR BUILDING WEALTH

Understand wealth
The first stage, according to Nash, is to understand wealth: why it's essential, how to earn it, how to enhance it, and what causes it to decline. Understanding the route to financial stability is vital. "If you can obtain control of your money," Nash adds, "you can choose how you spend your life."

That involves diverting spending from the trappings of wealth, such as costly automobiles or luxury goods, to less apparent wealth-building vehicles, such as investment accounts. Nash knows the need for affirmation of accomplishment within the African American community. He views the demand for displays of riches — which may make individuals feel valued — as an after-effect of slavery.

"We receive that attention and that sensation of actual achievement. It's not enough to have it and nobody knows it," he argues.

He expresses the transformation in perspective as: "I'm going to start investing these gains, I'm not going to live these profits." It's the difference between seeming affluent and being wealthy. Nash emphasizes that you can't have both at the same time, and spending to seem affluent gets in the way of utilizing the money to produce more money.

He claims he feels African Americans don't require financial literacy, which he describes as knowing about compound interest, how to balance a checkbook, etc.

He wants his society to learn "wealth literacy": an awareness of how to build assets that rise in value and create income.

Make a wealth goal
Your wealth objective may be financial comfort, independence, becoming a billionaire (which Nash adds is not all that much money nowadays), or getting wealthy, which he defines as a net worth of $5 million or more.

You could even desire to become ultra-rich or a billionaire. At the absolute least, your aim should be financial independence when you retire, and having a defined purpose can help you design a strategy to get there.

Learning how to get wealthy has little to do with how much money you have today and a lot with how you approach your objectives.

Through a mix of paying off debt, budgeting, investing, and growing your income, you may enhance your chances of getting wealthy and meeting your financial objectives. The average age of billionaires is 57, demonstrating that many successful individuals create money over time via rigorous habits and financial savviness (particularly if you don't come from a rich family).

Let's take a deeper look at how to get wealthy and examine the actions that may set you up for future financial well-being.

Self-made affluent individuals don't get rich by chance. Instead, they generally take active efforts to generate money and grow wealth. If you're ready to take charge of your money, selecting and adhering to a step-by-step strategy frequently helps improve your wealth.

1. Identify your objectives
Before you get started on being wealthy, establish a financial strategy. Here are a few things you may ask yourself while you put your strategy together:

What does being wealthy mean? Is there a specific net worth I'd want to hit?
What is my monthly financial goal? Am I seeking to put money away to invest or to pay off debt?

Am I seeking to reach early retirement? Get detailed with your replies so you know your exact aims. Once you have your big-picture vision created, break it down into smaller short-term objectives that are simpler to attain. By constructing this plan, you should have a greater understanding of what your goal is and how to get there.

2. End your high-interest debt
Nothing pulls down your hard work like high-interest debt. Total consumer debt balances climbed 5.4% between 2020 and 2021, according to Experian, one of the three major credit agencies.

Debt with high-interest rates, such as credit card debt, may be tough to pay back. Not only are you paying the initial amount you borrowed, but you're generally paying significant interest rates as well.

To take control of your debt, start by listing all your debts from highest interest rate to lowest. Consider making additional payments toward the initial loan amount on your high-interest loans first to decrease the total amount of interest you could incur by the time the debt is paid off. You'll likely need to explain that the additional payment is for the original loan amount – ask your lender if there is a set protocol you should follow when utilizing this technique.

Tip
Paying off debts with greater interest first is known as the debt avalanche approach, whereas paying off the loans with the lowest sum first is known as the debt snowball method.

Once you've paid off the first obligation in full, go on to the loan with the second-highest interest rate. You're paying less money on interest charges and retaining more money in your pocket by targeting high-rate loans.

3. Start planning and saving money
To pay off debt and reach your financial objectives, it's necessary to understand how to manage your money. Follow these steps to develop a basic budgeting plan:

Identify costs: Write down your revenue streams and costs and determine how much you earn or spend on average for each item on your list.

Keep track of important expenditure categories: Examine how much you spend each month on categories such as rent, utilities, and food. Don't forget to include an account for discretionary expenditures, such as dining out or purchasing a new book.

Look for places to improve: Once you have a bird's-eye perspective of your monthly financial flow, locate spots where you can cut down to save additional money.
Maybe you can cook at home more frequently than going out to restaurants. Or maybe there are free things you can do in your region to spend less on entertainment. Use the funds you generate to construct an emergency fund, develop a nest egg, pay off debt, or even invest.

4. Avoid Unnecessary Spending and Debt
Stop purchasing items you don't need.
Before you touch your card, ask yourself the following:

"Is this something I need?"
"Do I have anything comparable already?"
"Do I want this more than I want to become a millionaire?"
Every dollar you spend on something you don't need is one less dollar you can invest. Here's a reality check. If you invest an extra

$25 a week for the same 40 years, you would end up owning an additional $277,693.

Can you eliminate $25 of wasteful spending out of your weekly budget? Maybe, maybe not. But if you can, it will go a long way toward helping you attain your objective.

5. Pay yourself first
Without adequate money for emergencies, you risk getting into a bad financial place if an unforeseen bill happens. If you don't have cash on hand, you may charge the expenditure to your credit card or take out a loan, further hurting your finances by increasing your debt.

You enhance your savings, be sure to pay yourself first. This includes putting aside a part of your monthly income to put into a savings account, so you don't spend it elsewhere.

You may even automate this procedure so that it's done before the money becomes ready to spend.

You might set up an automated transfer from your checking account to a savings account. If your company employs direct deposit for your paycheck, you may opt to split the deposit, with a part of your paycheck going immediately into a savings account and the remaining in your checking account.

Tip
The greatest savings accounts frequently enable you to earn interest on your balance that is many times greater than the national average, enabling you to generate passive income and grow your money quicker.

6. Start investing as soon as possible
Investing your money is frequently one of the greatest methods to increase wealth over time, given that your investments are

successful. If you maintain all of your money in a basic bank account, you risk depreciating your cash owing to inflation. Investments are generally a wiser method to save.

Invest in stocks, mutual funds, or exchange-traded funds (ETFs) to enter the market as early as possible and take advantage of the potential of compound returns.

For example, let's imagine you invest $1,000 every month beginning at age 30. With a 7% rate of return, you'd have over $170,000 after 10 years, $500,000 after 20 years, and $1.15 million after 30 years. The sooner you invest, the more time you have to gain compound interest.

There are two primary account kinds for investing money in the stock market:

You may utilize tax-advantaged retirement plans, such as an employer-sponsored 401(k) or an IRA.
You may utilize one of the finest brokerage accounts like Stash, Betterment, or SoFi. Legendary investor Warren Buffett advocates starting with a diversified portfolio by adding ETFs that reflect key stock market indexes, such as the S&P; 500.

If you contribute to a 401(k) plan, take advantage of any company match advantages on a part of your contributions. The matched amount offers an instant 100% return on your investment, so it's worth maxing it up whenever feasible.

You may also cherry-pick stocks, bonds, and other investment vehicles, however, this may raise your risk and impair your investing plan.

Tip

Investing always carries some risk, but if you invest for the long-term, you may be able to weather the ups and downs of the market and still come out on top.

7. Increase your income
There's just so much money you can save with the salary you have. If you want to speed up your debt payback and raise your investment contributions, search for methods to produce money and increase what you earn. For example:

If you are pleased with your present employer: Consider asking for a raise or working for a promotion. Speak with your boss about your professional objectives and find out what measures you may take to develop towards them.

If you are open to searching for a new job: Consider taking a course or gaining a certification that can put you in the running for a position with better compensation. Make careful to negotiate any employment offer before accepting it.

Aside from your principal income, you might also explore one of the greatest side hustles. Whether you drive for Uber, freelance online, or establish a blog, there are numerous inventive ways to leverage your ability and entrepreneurial zeal into additional revenue.

8. Have the appropriate mentality
If you're accustomed to financial hardship, you may not feel that getting rich is conceivable for you. This limiting assumption makes every other step much more difficult to attain.

That's why establishing a wealth-building attitude is crucial to know how to get wealthy. It may take consistent, intentional effort to be successful and grow your wealth.

This isn't to imply that there aren't disparities in society or that everyone starts at the same starting line. Certain individuals confront significantly higher institutional impediments than others, and some groups have traditionally been denied chances to earn wealth and pass it down to their children.

But if you feel that being wealthy is unattainable for you, you may not take the measures required to reach this objective. Cultivating an abundant mentality and letting go of limiting ideas benefits you in your attempts to generate riches.

How long does it take to get affluent? Becoming affluent implies various things to different individuals. Some may feel affluent by accumulating a net worth of a million dollars or more. Others may be striving for financial independence that enables them to retire early. How long it takes to grow wealthy depends on how you define "rich."

The average age of millionaires is 57, showing that most affluent individuals attain a net worth of $1 million or more near their retirement years. Rather than winning the lottery, many billionaires undoubtedly grew wealthy by saving and investing over many decades.

Some retirement gurus advocate saving enough to replace 70% to 80% of your pre-retirement income. So if you earn $100,000 per year, you'd need $70,000 to $80,000 per year in retirement. Using a retirement savings calculator will help you calculate how much you'd need to retire and when you can accomplish this goal.

While this becoming-rich technique doesn't bring instant satisfaction, and it may take many years to complete, it may put you up for financial security in your elder years.

Rich is a subjective word. While one individual can feel affluent on $100,000 per year, such an amount would be a tremendous fall from grace for Kim Kardashian or Elon Musk. If we define affluent as twice the median national household income of $67,500 in 2020, then a salary of $135,000 or more would make you rich by this definition. When contemplating what income will make you affluent, it's essential to think about your position and ambitions.

Can you get wealthy in 10 years?
You may be able to become rich in 10 years through a combination of saving money, increasing your income, setting up multiple income streams, investing, and just plain ol' getting lucky. You can also learn how to start a business to take charge of your income.

Avoid get-rich-quick schemes. These schemes tend to be very risky, and while a few investors may make millions on these, many more people lose everything they invest.

At what age did Elon Musk become a millionaire?
Elon Musk became a self-made millionaire in 1999 as a 27-year-old entrepreneur when he sold a web-software company for over $300 million. He then became a millionaire at the age of 41. Musk claims he owed $100,000 in school debts when he began his first start-up.

Bottom line
Learning how to get wealthy starts with identifying your overall objectives and then making short-term goals that progressively move you closer to these goals. Consider how paying off high-interest debt, saving money, investing for the future, and growing your sources of income may help you become wealthy.

While it may take time and dedication to become wealthy, the following strategies may help you take charge of your finances and expand your wealth over time.

Chapter 3
OVERCOMING OBSTACLES TO WEALTH

Most individuals would agree that their major financial ambition is to attain financial independence. Those who have previously attained financial independence might adjust that ambition to keep their financial independence. It is worth reviewing some of the significant hurdles to the fulfillment of those objectives and seeing how they may be overcome.

Spending and Saving

Saving arises from the delay of consuming now to be able to consume later. This is distinct from investing, which Warren Buffett describes as forgoing consumption today to have the opportunity to spend more at a later period. The consequence of the term is fascinating. Not only must investors keep the buying power of their savings (i.e. their savings must generate a return at least as big as the rate of inflation); they must improve that purchasing power while overcoming the numerous other hurdles to success.

The major hurdle to gaining or sustaining financial independence is spending. There is no doubt that for many individuals present spending takes priority over future consumption. For a young family, house payments and the expense of raising and educating their children to rate considerably higher than saving for their retirement far in the future. And it is appropriate that they rank higher. A little financial preparation, however, might be beneficial in deciding the sort of lifestyle that can be enjoyed today without jeopardizing the potential for future financial freedom.

Similarly, even someone who theoretically has more than enough cash to live comfortably for the remainder of his or her life might swiftly dissolve that financial stability if it is not managed effectively. Although probably an extreme example, former professional hockey great Theo Fleury said in his book Playing with Fire, that he blew through over $50 million earned throughout his playing career, primarily squandered on liquor, drugs, and gambling. Avoiding drink, drugs, and gambling is a good idea, but the main issue is to recognize what amount of expenditure is sustainable in your specific circumstances.

Taxes

One of the major yearly expenses made by most individuals is one that they can comfortably get by without — taxes. In Canada, income taxes may be due to up to 50% of the income generated, depending on the amount of income and the province of residency. For investors, the situation is a bit brighter as several sources of income (Canadian dividends, capital gains) are taxed at considerably lower rates. As also, capital gains are taxed only when a property is sold and the capital gain is recognized. Owning shares of good quality enterprises that can be kept for a long period is in some respects akin to having assets in an RRSP or RRIF which are taxed only when monies are withdrawn. There is no immediate tax advantage when shares are acquired outside of an RRSP but no tax is paid while they are held (we're disregarding dividends for example) and then ultimately sold, tax on the gain is at half the rate paid on an RRSP or RRIF withdrawal.

Several elements go into establishing the tax burden for every single person, based on the quantity and sources of income. While we prefer to think of taxes as a proportion of income (e.g. the 50% indicated above), to put it in perspective it might be good to think of them as a percentage of one's portfolio. The income tax originating from an investment portfolio would normally fall in a range of ½% to 3½ % of the portfolio value. Individuals with significant yearly RRIF withdrawals, considerable interest income, and regularly traded stock portfolios would fall in the top half of the range, and those with no RRIF income, minimal interest income, and seldom traded equities portfolios fall in the bottom part of the range.

Before you start thinking that we are discouraging the use of RRSP/RRIFs because of the high rate of tax on withdrawals, remember that while the Canada Revenue Agency will eventually want to receive its share of your RRSP contributions and investment gains, in the meantime your investment returns are tax-sheltered and are compounding over time. In essence, an RRSP offers you tax-free compounding of your after-tax contributions. That part of RRSP contributions are subsidized by tax reductions also build on a tax-deferred basis, but the CRA will ultimately tax that back. The RRSP continues to be an excellent saving and investment vehicle.

The only item that trumps the RRSP as a savings and investment tool is the newly launched Tax-Free Savings Account (TFSA) (TFSA). Although there is no tax deduction for donations, investment income and profits are never taxed, even when withdrawn. You may even withdraw money in one year and re-contribute it in another year, without affecting your contribution limitations for any year. The sole negative is the relatively small contribution limit of $5,000 per year for the years 2009 – 2012 and $5,500 in 2013 and later years (with periodic inflation adjustments) (with periodic inflation adjustments). One must also be above 18 in any year for which a donation is made. These restrictions are cumulative though, so a person who has never contributed to a TFSA may contribute up to $25,500 this year. The TFSA is a "slam-dunk" for anybody with any investment income.

Management Fees and Other Investment Costs

It's impossible to pick up the personal finance sections of the newspaper without reading another piece on the negative effect of investment fees on net investment returns. At Genova, we earn fees for the administration of investment accounts therefore we are anything but neutral on the topic. It is our conviction though, that like any other expense, the quantity spent is less essential than the value gained in return.

Other than possibly stuffing cash in one's mattress, no investment takes place without incurring some expense, either directly or indirectly. Even depositing to a bank savings account involves the indirect cost of the disparity between what the bank pays you in interest and what it obtains when it loans your money to someone else. In a more varied portfolio, charges include the transaction fees for completing the purchase and sale of assets, custodial costs for the safeguarding of investments, collecting investment income and arranging payment for purchases, and collecting the proceeds of sales. Even the do-it-yourself investor will suffer these charges, although they may be packaged into a commission or administrative fee.

For an individual wishing to delegate the functions of investment research (essentially, determining what companies to own and what to pay for them) and portfolio management (applying the results of investment research to individual portfolios to achieve defined goals), there is an additional cost.

The pundits are correct that paying a high fee for managing a portfolio that mirrors an index makes little sense since the same result can be obtained for a much lower price. We feel that there is tremendous benefit in consistently sensible investment research and portfolio management that reflects established financial goals. Ultimately, it is the customer who evaluates if the adequate value is gotten for the price paid.

Inflation

Inflation is undoubtedly the most insidious killer of investment gains. Recall that the notion of investing involves eating less now to spend more later. However, having more money may not enable you to eat more. When Genova opened its doors in the autumn of 2006 the bundle of goods and services underpinning the Consumer Price Index could be bought for $100. Now, nearly seven years later it would spend around $112 to acquire the identical basket. At that time, inflation was fairly moderate, averaging slightly under 2% each year.

Interestingly, if you had purchased one-year GICs, which, on average, paid 1.3% of annual interest during that time and reinvested the money generated, you would have around $109 today (before taking taxes into account), which would not buy you what $100 could have bought seven years ago.

Navigating the Obstacle Course

Those who wish either to acquire or preserve their financial independence must overcome the barriers that are thrown in their road. One must both save and invest enough to obtain independence or spend just that which will enable the upkeep of present riches. One must also earn enough to pay taxes on investment profits and cover the expenses of generating them. If we estimate that the combined effect of inflation, taxes, and costs will be to erode perhaps 4%-6% per annum of the value of a portfolio, it is easy to see why investments owned more than those required for liquidity must be oriented toward growth. While it is always worthwhile to seek ways of lowering taxes and other costs, the primary focus should be on achieving a good return.

In developing the growth component of a portfolio, it is also vital to avoid another hurdle that we have not before addressed - speculation. Taking a gamble on shares of junior resource exploration businesses or high-tech startup companies, for example, sometimes results in a jackpot return but more frequently results in a hard lesson learned.

Owning shares of persistently productive firms, bought at competitive prices has guaranteed that Genova clients have been able to comfortably cross the investing barriers over the previous seven years and we think they will continue to do so.

Chapter 4
STAYING WEALTHY

Why do we believe that when you make a lot of money, that means you are rich? What does wealth mean? The Dictionary defines rich as "having a great deal of money or assets; wealthy," but let's think about that for a minute. How are you spending your money? Just thought you may be producing a great amount of money doesn't always imply you are wealthy.

Capitalism is hard. But part of the reason this happens is that getting money and keeping money are two different skills.

Getting money requires taking risks, being optimistic, and putting yourself out there.

But keeping money requires the opposite of taking risks. It requires humility, and fear that what you've made can be taken away from you just as fast. It involves frugality and a recognition that at least part of what you've produced is related to chance, so previous success can't be depended upon to continue forever.

Not "growth" "brains" or "insight." The capacity to hang around for a long period, without wiping out or being forced to quit, is what makes the largest difference. This should be the cornerstone of your strategy, whether it's in investing or your career, or a business you own.

A common trap of high-income earners is that although they may be bringing in a lot of money, they are also spending a lot of money. There is this idea that they need to show off their money and enjoy their money, which often leads to overspending.

People often don't realize that instead of spending your money as it comes in, you can get your money working for you through investments, then earn passive income on those investments. When you have your money working for you and have your money creating even more money, that is the sweet spot.

The best-kept secrets to maintaining wealth:

1. Don't spend your money on depreciable assets
The largest depreciable asset people spend the most money on is our vehicles. It is tempting to purchase a beautifully branded, fully loaded luxury vehicle that will cost you close to six figures, if not more. Still, that money would be better invested and pay you a return on that investment.

2. Never spend more money than you earn
It's tempting to keep up with the Joneses and spend money on gadgets, luxury items that do not hold value, and "stuff" that you don't need, but if you are spending more money than you are making, that

accumulates debt, and debt costs money to carry. Your money would better serve you invested where it pays a return.

3. Compound interest is the eighth wonder of the world

When you invest your money and are earning interest on top of interest, your money grows at an exponential rate. However, the reverse is true when you are carrying debt. You pay money to have that debt at an exponential rate as well, and it eats up your money quickly.

4. Invest in a financial education

When you invest in yourself and learn how to manage your money, that return on investment will be enormous, given that you execute what you've learned.

There will be a high return on investment for years to come when you use the financial skills you have learned to manage your money better.

5. Invest and track your net worth
Track your net worth is the best way to measure your wealth. Your net worth = all of your assets (what you own) less all of your liabilities (what you owe) (what you owe). The higher your net worth number is, the richer you are. Your wealth lies in the assets you own, such as investments, assets such as rental properties, and anything you own that holds value for a long time.

6. Your net worth lies in your behavior around money
How you spend, save, and manage your money will determine how wealthy you are or will become. One of the connecting threads amongst the richest individuals is that they are not ostentatious about it. They have incredible amounts of money but are not commonly seen vacationing on the most expensive yachts, wearing flashy clothes, or living an excessive lifestyle. Take a good look at Warren Buffet's lifestyle.

7. Layout a strategy for success

Having a plan is by far the most important secret of all. A goal without a plan is simply a desire, thus for you to attain your financial objectives, you need to plan out your investments. When you plan and map out your goals, it's easier to measure your results against your goals and hold yourself accountable. Having a plan makes your goals actionable.

The bottom line is if you are not giving your financial plan the attention that it needs to build your wealth, it is time to do so. The return on that investment of time, money, and energy will multiply itself over the years and will likely be the best investment you have ever made for yourself and your financial future.

www.ingramcontent.com/pod-product-compliance
Lightning Source LLC
Chambersburg PA
CBHW050315220526
45465CB00005B/2005